THE GOOD FIGHT

THE GOOD FIGHT

THE FEUDS OF THE FOUNDING FATHERS
(AND HOW THEY SHAPED THE NATION)

ANNE QUIRK

ILLUSTRATED BY
ELIZABETH BADDELEY

Alfred A. Knopf
New York

THIS IS A BORZOI BOOK PUBLISHED BY ALFRED A. KNOPF

Text copyright © 2017 by Anne Quirk
Jacket art and interior illustrations copyright © 2017 by Elizabeth Baddeley

Visit us on the Web! randomhousekids.com

Educators and librarians, for a variety of teaching tools,
visit us at RHTeachersLibrarians.com

Library of Congress Cataloging-in-Publication Data
Names: Quirk, Anne, author. | Baddeley, Elizabeth, illustrator.
Title: The Good Fight : the Feuds of the Founding Fathers (and How they
Shaped the Nation) / Anne Quirk ; illustrated by Elizabeth Baddeley.
Description: First Edition. | New York : Alfred A. Knopf, [2017] | "This is a
Borzoi book"—Title page verso.
Identifiers: LCCN 2016024844 | ISBN 978-1-5247-0035-5 (trade) |
ISBN 978-1-5247-0036-2 (lib. bdg.) | ISBN 978-1-5247-0037-9 (pbk.) |
ISBN 978-1-5247-0119-2 (ebook)
Subjects: LCSH: Founding Fathers of the United States—Biography—Juvenile
literature. | United States—History—Revolution, 1775–1783—Biography—
Juvenile literature. | United States—Politics and government—1775–1783—
Juvenile literature.
Classification: LCC E302.5 .Q59 2017 | DDC 973.3092/2—dc23

The text of this book is set in 13-point Baskerville MT.
The illustrations were created using pen and ink.

Printed in the United States of America
August 2017
10 9 8 7 6 5 4 3 2 1

First Edition

To my patient children, Isabel,
Andrew, and Aidan

—A.Q.

To my fifth-grade teacher Mrs. Peck,
who was the first one to teach me
about the founding fathers

—E.B.

He means well for his country, is always an honest man, often a wise one, but sometimes and in some things, absolutely out of his senses.

—BENJAMIN FRANKLIN on JOHN ADAMS

I can feel for him no other sentiments than Contempt or Abhorrence.

—JOHN ADAMS on BENJAMIN FRANKLIN

CONTENTS

INTRODUCTION

★

They seem so sure of themselves, looking out at the twenty-first century from coins or dollar bills or big bronze statues. Their eyes are steady, their faces are calm, their backs are straight. Only their collars are ruffled. Washington and Jefferson. Hamilton and Franklin and Adams. These are some of the great men who together founded a great nation.

At least, that's how it looks to us now. But go back a couple of centuries, back to before those coins were minted and those statues were raised, back to before the United States was a nation. Back then, the founding fathers hadn't founded anything, and they weren't at all sure that they ever would.

All of them, even cocky Alexander Hamilton, doubted

themselves. All of them, especially cocky Alexander Hamilton, doubted each other.

The founding fathers argued about when to fight the English. They argued about how to fight the English. They tussled over taxes. They disagreed about foreign affairs. They fought each other in private. They fought each other in public. They used essays. They used whispers. One of them even used a pistol.

Some of the fights were settled in their own time. Some of them are still being fought in ours.

Good fights can be long and frustrating, full of disappointments and setbacks. But they are also exciting, especially when you win.

Nothing short of Independence,
it appears to me, can possibly do.

—GEORGE WASHINGTON

I feel the justness of our cause.

—KING GEORGE III

GEORGE WASHINGTON

 VS.

KING GEORGE III

THE WAR OF THE GEORGES

1789: London and New York

It hurts to be on the wrong side of history. Winners, like George Washington, have great cities named for them and spiky monuments built in their honor. Losers, like King George III, are the butt of jokes. They lose the respect of their people. They lose power.

They can even lose their minds.

In the summer of 1788, nearly seven years after he lost his American colonies, fifty-year-old King George III started acting very strangely. He did not, as some insisted, mistake an oak tree for the king of Prussia. But he did talk for hours on end to no one in particular, pausing only for the occasional breath. He stopped sleeping. He barked orders at people who were long dead or completely imaginary.

"I am going to be mad," he reportedly told one of his sons, then sobbed.

Physicians from across England were summoned to the palace. Leeches were attached to the king's forehead. His scalp was shaved and blistered. He was placed in a straitjacket, his legs tied to his bedposts.

Parliament discussed replacing King George with his oldest son, the prince of Wales. Few were enthusiastic about this idea besides the prince of Wales.

After several months of treatments, the king improved—probably despite his doctors' efforts, not because of them—and he was pronounced cured in March 1789, at least for a while. Parliament stopped discussing the possibility of pushing him off the throne. Balls were held in his honor. Queen Charlotte issued a "Prayer of Thanksgiving upon the King's Recovery." Even the French ambassador celebrated, despite France's long tradition of going to war against English kings.

George Washington, however, had other things on his mind.

He had just been elected the first-ever president of the United States. "I was summoned by my Country," he said in his inaugural address, given on April 30, 1789, "whose voice I can never hear but with veneration and love."

The country now summoning Washington was America. The voices he now loved were American. But his first country had been England. His first loyalty had been to King George's grandfather, George II. Long before George Washington was an American citizen, he was an English subject.

No wonder George III fell apart. One of his own had turned against him.

In the winter of 1732, King George II probably hadn't heard that a new George had just been born in Virginia, one of England's colonies on the other side of the

Atlantic Ocean. Like most kings, George II was a busy man. He ruled over a growing empire that reached from England to America, India, and Africa. He shared his power with a parliament, an assembly of lawmakers who were elected by the English people. He also had nine children of his own, including an especially troublesome eldest son.

But George II didn't need to know little George Washington personally to know that the baby was English. The baby's parents, Mary and Augustine Washington, were English, too, and so were their neighbors along the Potomac River. The colonists up in Massachusetts were English. The colonists down in Georgia were

English. America was just another place where English people lived. That's what the king thought. That's what most people in America thought.

Little George Washington grew up sitting on English chairs and eating off English plates. He pulled English-made pants over his lanky legs. He would have been educated in England, too, as his older brothers were, if his father hadn't died young.

When Washington was in his early twenties, he served as an officer in the army of King George II. England and its longtime enemy France were at war, battling each other in Europe and in North America, where France had colonies of its own. In America, the conflict came to be called the French and Indian War. In Europe, it's known as the Seven Years' War. No matter its name, the war ended with an English victory.

The young American colonel won fame on both sides of the Atlantic for his bravery. By now, King George II knew the name George Washington. So did his grandson, King George III, who took the throne after his grandfather's death in 1769. (His father, the trouble-making eldest child of George II, had died earlier, much to the relief of many.)

Washington resigned from the army after five years and married a wealthy widow, Martha Custis. He inherited land and slaves, and he grew richer and richer. His property stretched far into the American wilderness. He was elected to the Virginia Assembly, where he mostly kept his mouth shut during political debates. But he was tall and strong, and heads turned whenever he walked into a room.

As the years passed quickly for George Washington, something inside him was slowly changing.

The more he thought about his king and the English parliament, the less he respected them. Their taxes were unfair. Their laws were unjust. They were keeping the best western lands for themselves. The more Washington saw of the vast North American continent, the less attached he felt to a small island in a distant corner of the North Atlantic.

By 1775, George Washington realized that he wasn't English, not anymore, and neither was anyone else in America.

Philadelphia and London: June 1775

On June 19, 1775, the Continental Congress asked George Washington to be general and commander in chief of the army of the United Colonies. He said yes because he believed that independence was worth the fight, but he wasn't happy about leading that fight.

AMERICA! AMERICA!

Representatives from the thirteen colonies had come to Philadelphia, the biggest city in North America, to discuss the future of America. Battles between the colonists and English soldiers had broken out around Boston, fueled by long-simmering disputes over taxes and civil liberties. More battles were coming. America needed its own military leader. Only one man, the Continental Congress decided, was right for the job.

Washington wasn't so sure. "I do not think myself

MOTH-ER ENGLAND!

MOTH-ER ENGLAND!

equal to the Command I am honored with," he told his fellow congressmen.

No one likes a braggart, not now and certainly not back then, when it was considered very rude and very crude to boast about your achievements. Gentlemen in the late 1700s, especially gentlemen from fine old Virginia families like the Washingtons, spoke modestly about themselves if they spoke about themselves at all.

George Washington, however, wasn't being modest for the sake of modesty. He wasn't just pretending to be humble. He was telling the truth. The job *was* way too big for him. It was probably too big for anybody. In fact, as jobs go, it was nearly impossible.

Take another look at the title: general and commander in chief of the army of the United Colonies. It sounds like a powerful position, until you realize two unhappy facts: The colonies were deeply divided, not united, and there was no army, not yet anyway.

Some of the delegates at the Continental Congress, especially those from Massachusetts and Virginia, were pushing hard *for* independence from England. Some of the delegates, especially those from the middle colonies of Pennsylvania, New York, and New Jersey, were pushing hard *against* independence. Some of the delegates, unsure of what they believed, just felt pushed. The opinions of everyday colonists were just as divided.

The army that General Washington was supposed to lead was puny, undisciplined, and badly equipped. Compared to the thousands of well-trained, well-equipped soldiers King George already had in the colonies, the American forces were almost a joke.

Over in London, though, the king wasn't laughing. The thirty-seven-year-old monarch took his royal duties very seriously. He took himself very seriously. Besides, his feelings were hurt.

How could his sons and daughters in America not

see that their king was kind and loving? That his intentions were good? Didn't they realize George III was doing God's work here on earth?

Of course—yes, of course—the king knew there were sharp disagreements about the taxes the colonists owed their mother country. He was aware that some colonists were unhappy that they had no representatives in England's parliament. Up in New England, obviously, tempers had flared out of control. The king knew all that. He was not a stupid man, despite what some people said.

But it was wrong, King George III believed, dead wrong, for some hotheaded farmers in tiny Massachusetts villages like Lexington and Concord to shoot and kill English soldiers. These soldiers were good and honorable men. They were peacekeepers, protecting the life and property of the colonies. They were patriots, not villains. Surely the colonies would come to their senses eventually. Cooler heads will soon prevail, George III assured himself.

Unfortunately for the king, George Washington, despite his cool and controlled appearance, was firmly on the side of the hotheads.

Writing to a friend, he reasoned that America could either fight for its freedom or be forever enslaved by England. "Can a virtuous Man hesitate in his choice?"

This virtuous Man didn't.

Still, the forty-three-year-old's military skills were rusty, to put it mildly. Nearly twenty years had passed since he was a colonel in the king's army, the same army he was now supposed to defeat. Back then he had commanded only a small band of soldiers. He had always been a leader, but he had never been a general.

Before he left Philadelphia to meet his troops in Boston, America's new commander in chief bought five horses and a carriage, and designed a uniform for himself. He also stocked up on a few books about military strategy.

In London, George III called the troublemakers in the colonies "unhappy and deluded." George Washington and his irksome army, His Majesty was certain, would be swiftly and soundly defeated by England's mighty military.

But just to be on the safe side, George III asked Parliament to ship more troops to America.

New Jersey and London: December 1776

Victory and defeat are flip sides of the same coin. The celebrated year of 1776, which started out so well for George Washington, was ending badly for the Americans. For that, King George III gave thanks.

In Boston, eight months earlier, George Washington had a short-lived opportunity to question his initial doubts. Maybe he *was* a military genius. Maybe the English *weren't* so tough. Maybe the fight would be short and sweet, a triumph for America!

On the morning of March 5, English troops had woken up to find hundreds of cannons staring right back at them. During the night, American soldiers had lugged heavy artillery up a bluff above the English encampment on Boston's harbor. It was a bold and daring move, and it worked like a charm. Less than two weeks later, the British departed Boston without firing another shot.

Then, in July 1776, the Continental Congress, in Philadelphia, declared America a new nation, free and fully independent of England and King George III. The Declaration of Independence was read aloud to the American army, who cheered loudly and whooped it up, perhaps a little too much. One band of soldiers sliced the head off a statue of George III, then paraded the severed body part around lower Manhattan.

George Washington told them simmer down.

By the autumn of 1776, though, no one in the American army was celebrating. Thousands of soldiers had been killed in a series of losing battles in and around New York City. Thousands more had deserted, leaving Washington desperate for more men. Some New Yorkers were even joining the British army, certain that the American cause was doomed.

That must have felt like a kick in the teeth for Washington. Before his troops, he appeared calm and confident. Privately, America's general was getting more and more gloomy. As he wrote his cousin Lund Washington on December 17, 1776, "I wish to Heaven it was in my power to give you a more favorable Acct of our situation," but unless a new wave of soldiers joined the army immediately, "the game will be pretty well up."

Washington's woes pleased George III, although the king didn't gloat. That would be in very poor taste, and

England's king wanted to be known for his forgiving heart, not his grudges.

George III was a deeply religious man, a devout Christian. He served his country as both its monarch and as head of its church, the Church of England, which also had many followers in America. In the last weeks of 1776, he asked his fellow believers to join him in a prayer for his "unhappy deluded Subjects"—a favorite phrase of his—"in America, now in open rebellion against His Crown":

> [G]rant us . . . not only strength and courage to withstand them, but charity to forgive and pity them, to show a willingness to receive them again as friends and brethren, upon just and reasonable terms and to treat them with mercy and kindness.

George Washington was a member of the Church of England. He had been baptized into the church as a baby. He and Martha were married by a minister of the faith, and he often attended Church of England services. But in the last days of 1776, he wasn't looking for mercy or kindness from George III and his brethren. At least, not until he made one more surprise attack.

On Christmas night, Washington led 2,400 American soldiers across an ice-choked Delaware River to raid a camp of British troops in New Jersey. The strike was daring, maybe even desperate, but it succeeded. Only two Americans died in combat, while hundreds of their opponents were taken captive. A valuable trove of British muskets, bayonets, and cannons was now in the grateful hands of the weapon-starved American army.

In those last days of 1776, three new facts came to light:

- King George III's prayers hadn't been answered.
- General George Washington's worst fears hadn't been realized.
- The Revolutionary War was far from over.

Chesapeake Bay and England: November 1781

George Washington was forty-nine years old in the fall of 1781. He had been general and commander in chief for six grueling years. He never had enough soldiers. He never had enough ammunition. He was tired. He was homesick. He was getting old, for heaven's sake.

King George III had his own passel of problems. The drawn-out American war had become unpopular in Parliament and throughout his kingdom. It was expensive, maybe wrongheaded, too. Maybe the American colonies *should* be an independent nation. Maybe England would be better off *without* its rebellious American colonies.

George III strongly disagreed, but even a king can't ignore the wishes of his people forever. George Washington and his troops might be unhappy and deluded, but they weren't giving up.

The war had begun in New England, then headed south. For a time, New York, New Jersey, and Pennsylvania saw the heaviest fighting. Later, the Carolinas and Virginia had their bloody turns.

In the summer of 1781, an army of 7,000 English soldiers led by General Charles Cornwallis started rebuilding a fort above the York River in Virginia. To protect them, English ships patrolled nearby on Chesapeake Bay.

New York City had long been rumored to be the site of the next big battle of the war. British commanders were convinced that Washington was still stung by his defeats there. They believed that the American general's pride demanded a victory on the site of his greatest failure.

The rumors were true, as it so happened, and they came from the most reliable source: George Washington himself. The defeat in New York *did* gall him. He *did* yearn to win it back. Again and again, he drew up detailed battle plans for attacking the British troops there.

The French general Rochambeau, however, thought that was a terrible idea. So did Admiral de Grasse, another Frenchman. They argued that the English would be much easier to defeat in the south, on Chesapeake

Bay. They insisted a great battle should be fought there, not in New York.

Wait a minute! Why were the French butting in? Why should Washington care what Rochambeau and his pal de Grasse thought? Wasn't this *America's* war of independence?

Oui, but also *non.*

Oui, because yes, America was fighting for its independence.

Non, because no, it wasn't *just* America's fight anymore.

France had joined the war in 1778 after much pleading from the Americans, especially Benjamin Franklin. The clever Pennsylvanian reminded the French that joining the American fight would be a new way to humiliate the English. There was little that the French enjoyed more than defeating another English king. For centuries, the two countries had been each other's favorite enemy. France was still peeved about losing the French and Indian War.

Working in secret, George Washington and his French partners planned a joint military operation. Their goal was to win a big battle so decisively that the English would finally give up and go home for good.

King George III shrugged off the threat. "The hands of France," he wrote, "are too full to be able to give any solid assistance to America."

By late September 1781, however, 16,000 French and American soldiers were closing in on the English troops in Yorktown. Admiral de Grasse and his French fleet had already thumped the British ships in the Chesapeake.

For the next few weeks, the English were bombarded by cannon fire and gunfire and surrounded on all sides. General Cornwallis begged for help that never came. He couldn't feed his horses. He could barely feed his men. A last-ditch effort to escape by sea failed utterly.

On October 17, a drummer appeared on the battlefield, followed by a British officer waving a white flag. The army of King George III was surrendering to the army of George Washington.

A peace treaty would take more than a year to write, but the fight was over. America had humbled the richest and most powerful empire in the world. The war between the Georges had ended with a historic victory.

The winner was obvious to all, and so was the loser.

I am, Honoured Sir, Your ever
dutiful Son.

> **—WILLIAM FRANKLIN
> to BENJAMIN FRANKLIN**

I have lost my son.

> **—BENJAMIN FRANKLIN
> on WILLIAM FRANKLIN**

BENJAMIN FRANKLIN

VS.

WILLIAM FRANKLIN

Philadelphia: 1726

When Benjamin Franklin was twenty, he decided to make himself perfect.

It was an ambitious goal, but then again, he was an ambitious young man, one of the most ambitious men in all the colonies. He had already learned the trade of printing, run away from Boston, and moved to Philadelphia. He had begun to make a name for himself as a writer, an inventor, and a scientist. He had even crossed the Atlantic, working in London for eighteen months. Now that he was back in Philadelphia, Franklin was ready to start a family and a business, and to train himself out of the bad habits he had picked up over the years.

He drew up a list of the twelve most important virtues. When a friend suggested a thirteenth, *Humility*, Franklin wasn't too proud to add that, too. Each virtue, he decided, would take him a week to master. If he tackled one virtue at a time, he would be a completely virtuous man in less than four months.

That was the plan anyway.

Temperance and *Silence*, the first two items on his list, were a cinch. Franklin was not in the habit of eating or drinking too much, at least not as a young man, and he knew how to hold his tongue. All clever people know that, and no one ever doubted the cleverness of Franklin.

Order, the third virtue, was tougher.

As Franklin wrote many years later in his *Autobiography*, perhaps with a huge grin on his face, "I was surprised to find myself so much fuller of faults than I had imagined."

Printing was a messy profession. Writing wasn't much neater. Ideas aren't tidy. And neither was Franklin. A week, a month, a year, perhaps even a lifetime, wouldn't be long enough for Franklin to become a completely orderly person.

He also had trouble with virtue number twelve, *Chastity*.

Sometime around 1730, although the exact date

isn't known for sure, Benjamin Franklin became a father. William Franklin was the name he gave the boy, but no one knows the name of William's mother. She was certainly never married to Benjamin Franklin. Deborah Read, who became Franklin's wife soon after the birth of William, never pretended to be the boy's mother, but she raised him with the two children she and Benjamin Franklin later had.

Perhaps William himself never even knew his mother's identity. His father, after all, knew how to hold his tongue.

Benjamin Franklin failed at moral perfection, but he succeeded at almost everything else he did in Philadelphia for the next twenty years.

His printing business boomed. The books, pamphlets, and newspapers that rolled off his busy presses found eager readers. *Poor Richard's Almanack,* an annual publication filled with practical advice and witty sayings—some written by Franklin and some collected by him—was a bestseller year after year.

He was appointed deputy postmaster of the colonies by order of the royal government in England. His fellow citizens elected him to the Pennsylvania Assembly.

He helped create a university, a hospital, and a library. All were thriving.

In his spare time, although exactly when that was is hard to imagine, he conducted important scientific experiments. William was at his side for many of them. Together, with the help of a key and a storm, they demonstrated that lightning was a form of electricity. This was a landmark scientific achievement, one of the greatest in the whole of the eighteenth century. Harvard, Yale, and the College of William and Mary awarded Benjamin Franklin honorary degrees. London's Royal

Society gave him the Copley Medal; it was the first time anyone outside England had been so honored.

In 1757, Benjamin Franklin was rich and famous. Now fifty-one years old, he had retired from the day-to-day running of his businesses. He had the time and the money to relax, to tinker with his inventions, to be with his family, his friends, and his books. He could take it easy.

But of course he didn't do that.

"God helps them that help themselves," or so said *Poor Richard's Almanack.*

So Benjamin Franklin, along with William, sailed away from Philadelphia that summer for England. He thought they might be gone for a year, maybe two. (In fact, except for two return trips to America, Benjamin ended up spending nearly thirty years on the other side of the Atlantic.)

Franklin had big plans for himself and for his son, now a handsome and clever man in his twenties. He had big plans for Pennsylvania, too. He was determined to strengthen the colony's ties to the king of England and weaken its ties to the Penn family.

Back in 1681, King James II of England paid off an old debt by granting land in America to William Penn and his descendants. The colony was called Pennsylvania, *sylvania* being a fancy name for "woods." "Penn's Woods," in other words. But seventy-five years later, Pennsylvania wasn't all woods anymore. Philadelphia certainly wasn't.

The colony should no longer be under the thumb of William Penn's children and grandchildren. Benjamin Franklin strongly believed that, and so did many other members of the Pennsylvania Assembly.

When one of William Penn's children heard about Franklin's intentions, he shrugged. "Mr. Franklin's popularity is nothing here," Thomas Penn said, referring to London. "He will be looked very coldly upon by great People."

Thomas Penn was right. The king's advisors, members of Parliament, and, not surprisingly, the Penn family mostly ignored the American. The "great people" in England didn't listen to his speeches. They didn't read his letters or his newspaper articles. They made him wait, sometimes for years, for meetings that went badly.

Despite all Franklin's efforts, the Penns kept their hold on Pennsylvania.

This, of course, was a disappointment, but Benjamin Franklin was not a brooder, and besides, he was having the time of his life in London. There was still work to be done for his colleagues back in the colonies, inventions to perfect, ideas to pursue, and new friends to make. Benjamin Franklin traveled, he wrote, he read. He added more honorary degrees to his collection. He was in no hurry to return to Philadelphia.

William Franklin was prospering, too. He studied law at the Inns of Court, where the sharpest legal minds in London instructed aspiring lawyers from around the empire. William and his classmates were taught that the English system of law was the wisest and the fairest in all the world and throughout all of history. At the heart of those wise and fair English laws, they were taught, was a wise and merciful English king.

William Franklin, an excellent student, learned his

lessons well. He revered the crown. He placed his king above all others.

Both Franklins made friends easily. But while the father preferred the company of scientists, philosophers, and writers, the son hobnobbed with the upper crust of English society. His crowd had grown up on country estates and in elegant London town houses. They had impressive titles, lots of money, and chummy relations with royalty.

When England's new king, the twenty-two-year-old George III, was crowned in 1760, William watched the ceremony with his fashionable friends from inside the magnificent Westminster Abbey. His father, who had no royal connections, settled for a spot outside.

William married on September 4, 1762. His wife was lovely and rich. She had been born in Barbados and educated in England, the daughter of a family who had made a fortune in the Caribbean sugar trade. A week later, William was appointed royal governor of New Jersey by George III.

Benjamin Franklin attended neither ceremony. He was on a ship back to America, having decided it was finally time to go home, at least for a while.

London and New Jersey: 1774

On January 29, 1774, a miserable Benjamin Franklin stood before the Privy Council, the king's most important group of advisors.

Scores of England's most prominent citizens watched his humiliation. The prime minister was in the audience. So was the archbishop of Canterbury, leader of the Church of England. Lords and ladies, dukes and duchesses, looked on, sometimes jeering at the aging American.

For nearly an hour, the king's lawyer, Alexander Wedderburn, called the world-famous sixty-eight-year-old a thief, a scoundrel, a liar, and worse. He claimed that Franklin had stolen private letters and then used those letters to rile up radicals and thugs over in Boston. Some of these hotheads, the lawyer reported, had recently disguised themselves as Indians and destroyed more than ninety thousand pounds of tea by dumping it into the city's frigid harbor.

A "wily American" is what Franklin truly was. He was just pretending to be loyal to the king. He was lying about his desire for peace and harmony in unruly Massachusetts. The truth, Wedderburn insisted, was that Franklin was actually "inflaming the whole province against His Majesty's government."

Franklin said nothing in his own defense, not one word. He was shocked. He was furious.

He was innocent.

At least, he told his friends that he was.

Yes, it *was* true that he had somehow gotten his hands on some old letters. The letters hadn't been written by Benjamin Franklin, and they hadn't been sent to Benjamin Franklin, either. They were written by Thomas Hutchinson, who became the royal governor of Massachusetts, and they were explosive. In them, Hutchinson fumed about the troublemakers in Massachusetts who were making his life miserable. He proposed limiting the legal rights of the colonists. Hutchinson had sent these letters to a friend in England. He never intended anyone else to read them.

How this correspondence came into Franklin's possession is a mystery. What he did with it is not. He sent the letters back to Boston, back to the very troublemakers that Hutchinson had railed against.

Why? Franklin claimed he did this to calm tensions,

not fuel them. He wanted the people of Massachusetts to know that shifty Hutchinson was the real enemy of their liberty, not good King George III.

Franklin had asked that the letters never be published. Was it his fault that they were?

Well, yes, it probably was.

After all, Franklin had been in the newspaper business. He knew a good story when he heard it. So did the radicals in Boston.

Benjamin Franklin feared that he might be arrested after the hearing, but he wasn't. He feared that his papers might be seized, but they weren't. He talked of going back to Philadelphia to be with his dying wife, but he didn't.

He did, however, write to his son, who had been living in New Jersey for a decade. "I wish you were settled in your farm," the elder Franklin wrote, encouraging William to start a new career in agriculture. "'Tis an honester and more honourable" occupation, he suggested, than his son's current line of work.

The royal governor of New Jersey thought otherwise. He had no intention of trading his mansion in bustling Perth Amboy for a farmhouse out in the sticks, but he did encourage his father to return home to America. "Your popularity in this country," William Franklin explained, "is greatly beyond what it ever was. . . . You may depend, when you return here, on being received with every Mark of Regard and Affection."

But this wasn't the only letter that Governor Franklin sent to London that week. He wrote the following to a close advisor of King George III: "His Majesty may be assured that I will omit nothing in my power to keep this province quiet."

He added: "No attachment or connections shall ever make me swerve from the duty of my station."

The royal governor of New Jersey was assuring his friends in London that his first loyalty would always be to his king, not to his father.

Paris: 1776–1784

William Franklin was absolutely right about his father's popularity. When the elder Franklin returned to Philadelphia in May 1775, the church bells of the city sounded in his honor. Benjamin Franklin was immediately appointed one of Pennsylvania's representatives in the Continental Congress. Conveniently, it was meeting just a few blocks from his house.

Would Benjamin Franklin join the delegates who were pushing for independence? Would he be among the delegates urging caution? Opinion at the congress was sharply divided, and no one knew where the great Franklin stood.

He wasn't saying, not at first.

John Adams, the sharp-eyed and sharp-tongued representative from Massachusetts, who was thirty years younger than Benjamin Franklin, noted that his elderly colleague could often be found "sitting in silence, a great part of the time fast asleep in his chair."

Several delegates feared that loyalty to King George III, not old age, was the reason that Benjamin Franklin kept so quiet. He had, after all, lived in London for such a very long time. The younger Franklin had already declared his opposition to American independence. Maybe the elder Franklin agreed with his son.

Benjamin Franklin decided to settle the matter by writing a letter to one of his best friends in London, William Strahan. "Mr. Strahan," he began.

You are a Member of Parliament, and one of that Majority which has doomed my country to Destruction. You have begun to burn our Towns and murder our People. . . . You and I were long friends; You are now my Enemy, and I am,

Yours,
B. Franklin

William Strahan never received the letter because it was never sent to him. In fact, it was never even intended for him. The letter was written for the delegates of the Continental Congress, and Franklin made sure that all of them read it. (Benjamin Franklin's real letters to Strahan were quite pleasant, even as the Revolutionary War dragged on.)

His approach may have been roundabout, but his message was clear. I'm for independence, Benjamin Franklin was announcing. I'm for revolution.

Soon Franklin was too busy for naps. He journeyed up to Boston to help the new commander of the Continental Army, General Washington, organize a ragtag collection of farmers and shopkeepers into a disciplined army. He trudged all the way up to Montreal to see if the British could be pushed out of Canada, too.

Back in Philadelphia, he helped a brilliant young Virginian, Thomas Jefferson, polish his draft of the Declaration of Independence.

A little more than a year after returning home to America, Benjamin Franklin sailed away from it again. This time he was headed for Paris, where he would try to persuade the French, who had long been at odds with England, to join America's fight against their common enemy.

Already famous in French scientific circles, Benjamin

Franklin quickly found fame in every corner of the French capital. No party in Paris was a success without him. No hostess was happy without him by her side. Paintings, prints, engravings, snuff boxes, and signet rings featuring his balding head and ample belly became the height of fashion in the world's most fashionable city.

"Your father's face," he joked to his daughter, has become "as well known as that of the moon."

But while his father was lighting up the French sky, William Franklin was locked up in an American prison. He had been imprisoned since the summer of 1776, by order of the Continental Congress.

What crime had William Franklin committed?

None. That's what the younger Franklin believed, unless it was a crime to do your job. "It is His Majesty's express Command," the royal governor had been informed, "that you do exert every Endeavour and employ every means in your power, to aid and support him."

To William Franklin, this meant urging the citizens of New Jersey to stay loyal to their king. It meant ignoring all declarations of independence coming from Philadelphia. It meant keeping track of troop movements. It meant reporting on the travels of prominent revolutionaries, like his father.

The royal governor of New Jersey did these things to keep the peace. He was an honorable man, he insisted, a loyal servant to his people and to their king.

No, said the Continental Congress. You are a traitor.

And his father, a member of that congress, didn't disagree.

For nearly three years, William Franklin was held captive by people who were once his friends and colleagues. Some of that time was spent in solitary confinement in the harshest prison in America. He never asked for help from his famous father, and he was never given any.

When he was released in exchange for an English prisoner, William Franklin moved to New York City, which was under the control of the king's army. It was a safe place for people like him. People, that is, who hadn't abandoned George III. People who believed that America would never win its war of independence.

People, as it turned out, who were wrong.

Soon after the English troops surrendered to George Washington in Yorktown, William Franklin and thousands of other loyal English subjects realized that they had no future in an independent America. In the summer of 1782, William sailed for England.

Two years later, he wrote his father, who was still in Paris.

"Dear and Honoured Father," the younger Franklin began. "I have been anxious to write to you, and to endeavour to revive that affectionate Intercourse and Connection which till the Commencement of the late Troubles had been the Pride and Happiness of my Life."

Would they be able to see each other? William Franklin wondered.

The war was over. The peace treaty with England had been signed.

"I ought not to blame you," the father replied, "for differing in Sentiment with me in Public Affairs. We are Men, all subject to Errors." But he added emphatically, *"[T]here are Natural Duties which precede political ones."*

You have a right to have your own political opinions, Benjamin Franklin was saying to William, but a son's first duty is to his father, not to his king.

The seventy-eight-year-old added that now was not a good time for a visit. Maybe later.

A year passed before Benjamin Franklin, stopping in England on his way back to Philadelphia, finally saw William. Their reunion was brief. No fences were mended. No apologies were accepted. No forgiveness was granted. The son stayed in England. The father spent the last four years of his life in America. They would never see each other again. They never exchanged another letter.

Although he lived his entire life in the eighteenth century, Benjamin Franklin is still America's favorite can-do guy. When he decided that chimneys were wasting heat, he invented the Franklin stove. When he was tired of taking off one pair of glasses and putting on another, he invented the bifocal lens. When he realized that his country needed its independence, he joined with others to invent the United States of America.

But his break with his son also reminds us just how destructive political fights can be, especially within families. Sometimes the damage is so great that no one can fix it, no matter how clever he is.

I am a stranger in this country.
I have no property here, no
connections.

—ALEXANDER HAMILTON

He hated every man, young or
old, who stood in his way.

—JOHN ADAMS
on ALEXANDER HAMILTON

ALEXANDER HAMILTON

 VS.

HISTORY

In the early morning of July 11, 1804, Alexander Hamilton fought a senseless duel with Aaron Burr.

Hamilton, formerly secretary of the Treasury, a top aide to General George Washington, and the brightest clerk on the island of St. Croix, was now one of the best lawyers in New York City. He was a newspaper publisher, too, yet another accomplishment in his long list of impressive achievements. His marriage wasn't perfect, but it was happy, and he was the father of eight. The family lived in a grand house on a hill in what was then the countryside of upper Manhattan.

Burr was the vice president of the United States,

officially anyway, but he was on the outs with President Jefferson and had almost no power. (That happened often in the early years of the United States, and sometimes still does.) He was a widower with a grown daughter.

The two men had known, and disliked, each other for years. Both had fought in the Revolutionary War. Both were New Yorkers and lawyers. Both were political men, often on opposite sides of an issue. Hamilton was in the habit of saying insulting things about Burr. But that wasn't unusual for him. Hamilton was in the habit of saying insulting things about a lot of people.

So, surely, few took much notice when a newspaper in Albany reported on yet another incident of Hamilton's bad-mouthing Burr. This time, however, Burr demanded a public apology. Hamilton refused. Tensions rose, and one thing led to another. After a few months of negotiations, which left plenty of time for a clever man like Hamilton to find a way out of the duel if he had wanted to get out of the duel, the two men took their places on a high patch of land in Weehawken, New Jersey, right across the river from New York City.

Dueling was illegal in both states, but officials in New Jersey had a reputation for looking the other way. Burr is generally believed to have been practicing his shot in the days before the duel. Hamilton busied himself with letter writing.

"Apology," he wrote, trying to explain himself, "is out of the question."

Alexander Hamilton never could resist a fight.

The West Indies: 1757 (or 1755)–1772

"I wish there was a war," Hamilton wrote to his friend Edward Stevens in 1769. "I mean to prepare the way for futurity."

The boy who wrote that letter was twelve, or maybe fourteen. There is some evidence that Alexander Hamilton shaved two years off his age when he moved to New York as a teenager. (If that's true, he wouldn't have been the first New Yorker—or the last—to pass himself off as a bit younger than he was.)

Whatever the year, 1757 or 1755, Alexander Hamilton was born on the island of Nevis, a small dot in the West Indies, as the Caribbean region was then known. He was raised on Nevis and on nearby St. Croix.

When Hamilton was eight (or maybe ten), his father deserted the family. Three years later, his mother died. Hamilton and his older brother, James, were placed in the care of a grown-up cousin. Before long, the cousin was dead, too. Then James Hamilton went off on his own to become a carpenter's apprentice.

Having no home, no family, no money, and practically no education is a miserable way to start your teenage years, but Hamilton wasted no time moping. He was too busy.

St. Croix was a small place, but it certainly wasn't sleepy in Hamilton's day. Enormous fortunes were being made on the island. Its climate was perfect for growing sugar cane, and the world was beginning to acquire a sweet tooth.

Ships sailed into St. Croix's harbors with full cargoes of mules, bricks, books, rope, and more, from all over the world, then sailed away stuffed with sugar. Sailors came ashore speaking French, English, Spanish, and Dutch, and from time to time, especially during drunken brawls, cursing in those tongues as well. Murderous pirates lurked offshore. Duels were common.

Chances are, Alexander Hamilton was seldom bored.

Finding a job as a clerk at Beekman and Cruger, one of the best trading companies on the island, he soon learned almost everything there was to know about the business of buying and selling. He took note of all the incoming ships and their cargo. He mastered the art of dealing in British pounds or Danish ducats or Spanish pieces of eight or whatever currency was offered. He was never cheated and he didn't cheat others. Even his penmanship was superb.

In 1771, after Mr. Beekman left the firm and Mr. Cruger went to New York for five months, Alexander Hamilton ran the business on his own. No one seemed to think he was too young for the job. Alexander Hamilton certainly didn't.

Still, the teenage striver was restless. He yearned for greater challenges, bigger worlds. He wanted to be a hero. He wanted to be important. He knew that history never favors office clerks, no matter how beautiful their handwriting.

On the last day of August 1772, a massive hurricane slammed into the island and its Caribbean neighbors. It wasn't the war that Alexander Hamilton was hoping for, but it was as devastating.

"Good God! what horror and destruction," he exclaimed in a letter that appeared in the *Royal Danish American Gazette,* a leading newspaper on St. Croix. "It seemed as if a total dissolution of nature was taking place."

The letter was an immediate sensation, read and praised throughout the island, including by the governor himself. A fund was quickly established to send the talented young man to North America, where he could receive the formal education he so richly deserved.

Hamilton promptly departed his small island, never to return.

Valley Forge, Pennsylvania: 1777–1778

In the winter of 1777–1778, Alexander Hamilton was barely into his twenties, yet he was already well on his way to becoming one of the most important people in America.

Four years earlier, a few weeks after his ship landed in Boston, Hamilton enrolled at Elizabethtown Academy, a college preparatory school in New Jersey. Six months later, convinced that he was sufficiently prepared, he started at King's College (now Columbia University) in New York City. His course load was absurdly heavy, yet in his spare time he studied military history and learned the ins and outs of guns and cannons. He got interested in politics. Soon he was writing political essays for the leading newspapers of the day.

This child of the tropics even managed to get used to cold weather.

That was important if you were a soldier in the woods of Pennsylvania, as Hamilton was that awful winter. He abandoned his studies and joined the fight for American independence in 1776. After rocketing up the military

ranks—everything Hamilton did, he did quickly—he
was now a top aide to General George Washington.

The eyes of the world were now fixed on Washington and on Britain's thirteen colonies along the Atlantic seaboard. This was exactly the sort of opportunity
Hamilton had longed for back when he toiled in a small
office on a small island. He was finally in the right place
at the right time.

Trouble was, Colonel Hamilton feared that his side
was losing, and he wasn't the only one fretting. General
Washington also worried that an American defeat was
at hand. The British were all but counting on it.

In the miserable winter of 1777–78, the Continental Army of America was camped outside the Pennsylvania village of Valley Forge, on the verge of collapse. The soldiers were sick, hungry, and barely clothed. Thousands were dying. Thousands were already dead.

George Washington, the most powerful man in America, felt powerless. Two days before Christmas 1777, in a despairing letter to the Continental Congress about the suffering of his troops, he wrote, "[F]rom my Soul [I] pity those miseries, which it is neither in my power to relieve or prevent."

In Philadelphia, just twenty miles away from Valley Forge, the British army was enjoying its fill of good American food and warm American beds. Many Philadelphians—and many other Americans, too—were proud to be British citizens. They had no desire for independence. In fact, they thought it was a terrible idea.

Many other Philadelphians didn't have strong opinions about politics one way or the other. They were just happy to be paid in sound British pounds, rather than the nearly valueless American money.

The Redcoats decided to stay put until the weather improved. They were sure they could defeat a weak Continental Army once spring came around. Until then, they would wait.

But America couldn't wait, and neither could Hamilton. Patience was never his strength.

General Washington and his aide were proud men, although not too proud to beg Congress, or anyone, for help. "For God's sake," Hamilton wrote a fellow officer, detailing the troops' desperate need for food, horses, medicine, wagons—for almost everything. "Our distress is infinite."

Eighteen months earlier, the future had seemed so bright. The summer of 1776, when the Continental Congress voted unanimously in Philadelphia to form a new nation, had been full of high hopes and brilliant speeches.

Now most of those big talkers were long gone. John Adams and Benjamin Franklin were overseas looking for foreign aid and foreign fighters. Thomas Jefferson was on his mountaintop estate in Virginia. John Hancock and his impressive signature were back in Boston.

Congress wasn't even in Philadelphia anymore. After the British army marched into the city, the seat of America's government had moved to York, Pennsylvania, a farming town eighty-eight miles away from Philadelphia. For some, it might as well have been eighty-eight thousand miles away. Many congressmen didn't bother to make the trip. At one point in late 1777, only nine were actually present in York.

The major problem with the new national government in America was that there was no national government in America, or not much of one anyway.

The Continental Congress had almost no money in its treasury, no reliable way to collect money, and no control whatsoever over the individual states. How could a few men in a small village far away from almost everything save a starving army? What power did they have?

Very little.

General Washington knew that, but still, with the help of his staff, especially Colonel Hamilton, he came up with a plan. Three congressmen, accompanied by three advisors, came to Valley Forge to inspect the camp. As soon as they dismounted their horses, they were handed a to-do list.

The writing was clear and direct. The penmanship of the twenty-one-year-old (or maybe twenty-three-year-old) colonel was superb.

"Something must be done," the report began. "Important alterations must be made." Among its recommendations: Officers should be given lifetime benefits; soldiers should be drafted from every state; punishment for bad conduct should be stiffened; rewards for success should be sweetened.

The Continental Congress got the message. "Important alterations" were made, and over time Washington's army was stronger for those changes. The war effort was also boosted by some very good news that arrived from Europe in the spring of 1778. French ships, French soldiers, and French money were crossing the Atlantic to aid the rebellion.

Still, the war dragged on for three and a half more bloody years. Hamilton stayed in the army to the very end, until England surrendered in Yorktown on October 17, 1781.

The ambitious young man finally had his great victory. But he never forgot, and neither did Washington, just how close they—and all of America—had come to defeat.

New York and Philadelphia: 1789-1795

A new nation needs new laws, new institutions, new habits. It needs leaders with vision and citizens with patience. It needs money, too.

Americans spent eight years fighting England for its independence, and they spent even longer fighting among themselves to create a new national government. There was no bloodshed in this conflict, but there were plenty of battles. Some of them were very nasty. Many of them involved Alexander Hamilton.

When George Washington was inaugurated as the

first president of the United States, in 1789, the Revolutionary War had been over for several years, but its costs lived on. Loans from ordinary Americans had gone unpaid. So had loans from foreign governments. Soldiers were still waiting for the pay they had been promised.

The national government was in debt. State governments were in debt. Some states owed a lot of money. Some owed a little. The loan agreements were often confusing. It wasn't always clear to whom the debt was owed. It was all a big mess, as money problems often are.

Washington asked his former military aide to become America's first-ever secretary of the Treasury. The job was to untangle the country's current financial problems and then set it on a sound course for the future.

The task was huge. The pay was minimal. The hours were brutal. The position would take Hamilton away from his wife, their growing family, and his busy law practice. If he failed, his reputation would be ruined. If he failed, the United States might fail, too.

Of course Hamilton said yes.

"I conceived myself," he later explained, "to be under an obligation to lend my aid towards putting the machine in some regular motion."

This sounds modest. It wasn't. Hamilton believed that he was the best person to get the new government ("the machine") up and running. Almost immediately after taking office, he started making plans for the financial future of the United States. He presented a series of ambitious reports to Congress. More than two hundred years later, they are still considered to be brilliant and amazingly nervy.

This is what he wanted to do: take all the national debts and all the state debts and combine them into one great big debt. Then he wanted to create a national bank, the Bank of the United States, which would oversee the repayment of the nation's debts. The new bank would also make large amounts of money available for private business investments and public projects.

His goal was to build trust.

If the United States couldn't be trusted to pay its debts, no foreign government would lend money to the new nation, at least not at reasonable interest rates. No citizen would again volunteer to serve in its army. No business investor would risk money on new ventures.

Without trust, the United States of America would fail.

Unfortunately, trust was exactly what Hamilton was lacking from many of his colleagues, especially Thomas Jefferson.

Jefferson was a decade older than Hamilton. He was the principal author of the Declaration of Independence. After serving as governor of Virginia, then as a diplomat in Paris, he had been chosen by Washington to be America's first secretary of state. He was responsible for the new nation's relations with the rest of the world.

Thomas Jefferson was a very important man, much admired by other important men. Unfortunately for Hamilton, Thomas Jefferson didn't like banks very much, and he really hated bankers.

Jefferson believed that people should make their living from the land, either working as farmers themselves or as owners of plantations that were farmed by others.

(His estate, Monticello, was largely worked by enslaved men, women, and children.) He knew that banks were sometimes necessary, but he thought that too much money concentrated in the hands of too few people always led to corruption.

Thomas Jefferson was convinced that Hamilton would use the national bank to enrich himself and his pals in New York. (The Virginian didn't like New Yorkers very much, either.)

James Madison felt the same way. A dear friend to Jefferson, the congressman from Virginia had once been a close ally of Hamilton's, but no longer. Madison and Jefferson, an offended Hamilton told a friend, are "at the head of a faction decidedly hostile to me."

That was putting it mildly. In fact, Jefferson confided to Madison that any Virginian doing business with the new Bank of the United States should be found "guilty of high treason and suffer death accordingly."

It's unlikely that Jefferson was serious about executing bank customers. Words sometimes get away from writers, even brilliant ones like Thomas Jefferson. But he clearly despised the Treasury secretary's plan, and the man behind it. He encouraged newspapers to write awful things about Hamilton.

Alexander Hamilton fought back. Using a pen name that fooled no one, he published articles attacking the

secretary of state. Privately, he urged Washington to re-move Jefferson from his office.

Washington was not pleased.

It's hard enough to run a country without having your two most important cabinet officers continually at each other's throats. President Washington tried to make peace between Hamilton and Jefferson. He failed. Neither of them were the least bit interested in peace.

Worse, at least from Jefferson's perspective, President Washington tended to side with Hamilton. He supported the combining of the state and national debts. He supported the new bank. He believed, as Hamilton did, that a national government needed to be strong in order to survive.

They had learned that lesson together at Valley Forge.

In 1791, the Bank of the United States opened. It was an immediate success, just as Hamilton had predicted. Some cunning New Yorkers made a lot of money, just as Jefferson had predicted. But some of them lost it quickly, too.

Hamilton himself was short of cash. He was always more interested in other people's money than his own.

A disgusted Jefferson resigned as secretary of state in December 1793. An exhausted Hamilton resigned as Treasury secretary in January 1795. For the rest of their lives, neither man ever had a good word to say about the other.

Alexander Hamilton and Aaron Burr stood ten paces apart—about twenty-five feet—aimed their pistols, and then fired. Hamilton's bullet never touched Burr. It was later found in a nearby tree. Burr's bullet tore through Hamilton's abdomen before lodging in his spine.

When he found the strength to speak, Hamilton said, "This is a mortal wound." He was right, as usual. In addition to everything else that he knew, Hamilton knew a fair amount about the human body. His companions had enough time to row him back across the river and take him to the Greenwich Village home of a friend, but he died the next day, surrounded by family and friends.

The news of Hamilton's violent end shocked the nation. His funeral on July 14 was the largest Manhattan had ever seen. Shops were shuttered. Ships dropped their flags to half-mast. Tough-minded New Yorkers openly wept as Hamilton's casket slowly made its way to Wall Street's Trinity Church.

The scene at the church graveyard, observed the *New York Evening Post,* "was enough to melt a monument of marble."

Dying in a duel? Why would a man as brilliant as Hamilton do such a stupid thing? What was he thinking? No one knows for sure, despite all the best efforts of historians. Other people's thoughts are always difficult to read, especially when the thinker has been dead for two hundred years.

Perhaps Hamilton didn't really know.

The opening years of the nineteenth century had treated him cruelly. Not only had his greatest political opponent, Thomas Jefferson, become president in 1801, but America's purchase of the Louisiana Territory—a bold move that doubled the area of the United States in 1803—had made the tall Virginian wildly popular among his countrymen. That must have been hard for Hamilton to stomach.

Far worse, though, was the loss of his oldest son, Philip, who had died in a senseless duel of his own in 1801. The grief-stricken father became even quicker to anger. More and more, he was throwing himself into arguments, not just in the courtroom.

Alexander Hamilton was only forty-seven years old when he died. Or maybe he was forty-nine. Either way, he died much too young.

An immigrant, a self-made man, someone who had fought hard for everything he achieved in his life, Hamilton was probably the most American of America's founding fathers. He believed that America had always been more than thirteen English colonies on the far side of the Atlantic Ocean. It was one nation, indivisible, full of promise and bound for greatness. It was a place for people like him.

His ideas continue to spark furious debates. Was he right? Would the United States have collapsed without a strong national government and a centralized financial system? Was Jefferson right? Did a clever New York lawyer and his banking buddies get the country into the bad habit of borrowing and spending too much?

Alexander Hamilton would likely be thrilled to know that he is still stirring up arguments, even though it's been more than two centuries since he could join in. Surely the truest way to honor his legacy is to fight about it.

His soul is poisoned with Ambition.

—JOHN ADAMS
on THOMAS JEFFERSON

I think it a part of his character to suspect foul play in those of whom he is jealous.

—THOMAS JEFFERSON
on JOHN ADAMS

JOHN ADAMS

~ VS. ~

THOMAS JEFFERSON

THE FOUNDING FRENEMIES

When Congress sent Thomas Jefferson to Paris in 1784, Benjamin Franklin and John Adams were already there. They had been abroad for most of the Revolutionary War, trying to convince the old powers in Europe to support the creation of a new nation on the other side of the Atlantic. Along with John Jay from New York, the two men had negotiated a peace treaty in September 1783. It took several months for the Treaty of Paris to become official, but by the time Jefferson arrived in France, America was a fully free and independent country.

The Virginian was taking over the duties of Franklin, who was eager to get back home to Philadelphia. Franklin was suffering from gout and boils. He was tired. He was old.

He was also sick to death of his snappish colleague from Massachusetts.

"He means well for his country, is always an honest man, often a wise one," Franklin wrote of Adams, "but sometimes and in some things, absolutely out of his senses."

Adams held an even lower opinion of Franklin, whom he thought was lazy and spoiled by his great fame. "I can feel for him no other sentiments than Contempt or Abhorrence," Adams wrote to a colleague.

But both men admired Thomas Jefferson and his beautiful way with words. Back in 1776, when Jefferson was still a very young man, they asked him to write the first draft of the Declaration of Independence. When other members of the Continental Congress started amending the document—adding clauses here, dropping phrases there—Adams and Franklin comforted an unhappy Jefferson, who thought his work was being destroyed. (Jefferson was wrong. The Declaration of Independence is brilliant, maybe even better and stronger because of the changes. But still, no writer likes to be rewritten, especially by a committee.)

Forty-one years old when he landed in France, Jefferson was enthusiastic about serving his country in a new way. His term as governor of Virginia during the war had been stormy. His wife had died and so had several of their children. This was his first time in Europe, a chance to start over. He was eager to meet some of the world's most celebrated minds in one of the world's most beautiful cities. He also planned to go shopping.

Thomas Jefferson loved to shop..

He purchased books by the armload for himself and for his friends. He acquired paintings and sculptures. He rented a spacious house in the most fashionable district of Paris and filled it with carpets, sofas, chairs, candlesticks, and a great deal more. He bought fine food and expensive wine. He hosted elegant dinners and entertained elegant friends.

But Jefferson's most treasured friends in Paris were John Adams; his lively wife, Abigail; and their two oldest children—seventeen-year-old John Quincy, who had been abroad for many years with his father, and nineteen-year-old Abigail, who had recently arrived with her mother. The meals he most enjoyed were their simple family dinners, during which the widower and the spirited Adams clan traded gossip about mutual friends (and enemies). Together, they took in the city's splendid sights.

Paris, 1784

A little more than a year after Jefferson came to Paris, Adams was appointed ambassador to England. He moved to London.

"The departure of your family has left me in the dumps," Jefferson wrote to Adams on May 25, 1785. "My afternoons hang heavily on me."

A few years later, after both men returned to America and became political opponents, eventually running against each other for president, Abigail took a darker view of Jefferson. She was always fiercely loyal to her husband. The man she thought had been so kind and generous to her family now struck her as dishonest and scheming as a politician. She began to think of Jefferson as an enemy.

But in Paris, all she felt was affection.

"I shall really regret to leave Mr. Jefferson," she wrote her niece. "He is one of the choice ones of the earth."

Washington, D.C.: 1801

Before sunrise on March 4, 1801, when John Adams was still the president of the United States, at least for a few more hours, he left the President's House in Washington, D.C., took his seat on a public coach, and started home for Quincy, Massachusetts.

He chose not to stay in town for the inauguration of his successor, Thomas Jefferson. Many of Adams's political opponents and even some of his supporters thought he was being a sore loser. Some historians still do.

John Adams had been elected the second president of the United States in 1796, after serving eight years as vice president to George Washington. Thomas Jefferson had vowed to retire forever from public life after he resigned as secretary of state, but then he changed his mind. He was elected vice president, serving under President Adams.

The two men hadn't run as a team, and they didn't

govern as a team. They seldom spoke to each other. Months could pass without their even living in the same city.

The United States was barely into its teens during the years that John Adams was president, a very short time in the life of a country. Many important questions about the new nation were still being hotly debated. (Some of them continue to be hotly debated, two centuries later.)

Does a permanent army protect ordinary citizens, or does it give the national government too much power? When does some taxation turn into too much taxation? Can state governments ignore national laws they dislike? What is America's role in the larger world? Which countries are America's friends? Which are its enemies?

Jefferson and Adams almost never agreed on the answers.

In 1800, the two men ran against each other for president. Jefferson was far too polite (and clever) to publicly criticize Adams, but his supporters ignored such niceties. They wrote vicious stories about the current president, calling him such dreadful things as a "gross hypocrite," a "repulsive pedant," and a "strange compound of ignorance and ferocity, of deceit and weakness."

The thin-skinned man from Massachusetts seethed privately to his family and friends. No one likes to have mud slung at him. Besides, President Adams thought he had done a pretty good job, all things considered. The country was in good shape financially. A war with France had been averted.

The voters of 1800, however, wanted change. John Adams didn't just lose to Thomas Jefferson; he also lost to Aaron Burr. Due to a wrinkle in election laws back then, which was soon corrected, Jefferson and Burr had exactly the same number of votes in the electoral college, 73 to 73. For several tense months, it was uncertain who would be the next president of the United States. After the deadlock was finally broken, Jefferson was elected president and Burr was named vice president.

Adams's situation was the same either way. He was out of a job.

Still, he was proud of what he had accomplished. "I shall leave the State with its coffers full," the departing president wrote a friend, "and the fair prospect of a peace with all the world smiling in its face."

Adams had been the first president to govern from the brand-new city of Washington, D.C. He was the first president to live in the mansion that we now call the White House. He was the first president, and maybe the only one, to join a bucket brigade to put out a fire at the Treasury Building.

He was also the first president to be defeated for re-election.

There was no official role for him at his successor's inauguration. There was also no unofficial role for him. There is no evidence he was even invited to attend the inauguration. He certainly wasn't mentioned in Thomas Jefferson's speech.

Maybe the soon-to-be-former president of the United States meant no offense when he left Washington early on March 4, 1801. He never admitted to departing in anger, and he often owned up to his mistakes. It is possible that he simply wanted to catch the earliest coach back home to his beloved Abigail, who had left the capital months before.

That morning, perhaps Adams just thought of himself as an unemployed sixty-five-year-old with a long road in front of him.

Monticello and Quincy: 1812-1826

When you grow older, new friends are hard to make, but old enemies are easy to forgive.

On January 1, 1812, after nearly ten years without one word having passed between them, seventy-six-year-old John Adams sat down at his writing table in Quincy, Massachusetts, and penned a brief New Year's greeting to Thomas Jefferson at Monticello.

The reply from the mountaintop estate in Virginia came swiftly. "A letter from you," wrote the sixty-eight-year-old Jefferson, "calls up recollections very dear to my mind."

That was all it took, just one note. Old quarrels that once seemed important enough to split apart America were put aside. Old insults were forgotten, old rivalries ignored.

Two old men revived their old friendship.

In the early 1800s, before there were planes, cars, and even trains, the distance between Massachusetts and Virginia seemed greater than it does today. Neither of the former presidents had the desire or the strength to make such a grueling journey. They knew it was unlikely that they would ever see each other again. Time was now their common enemy. But they still had much to say, especially John Adams.

He assured Jefferson in 1813, when the Virginian worried about falling behind, "Never mind it, my dear Sir, if I write four Letters to your one; your one is worth more than my four."

Adams was being too modest. Both men wrote priceless letters, some of the wisest and kindest you will ever read. They reported on their aches and pains. They discussed Jefferson's plans for the new university he was creating in nearby Charlottesville, the University of Virginia. They mourned their losses, especially Abigail

Adams, who died in 1818. She may have lost her faith in Jefferson, but he never abandoned his fondness for her.

Mostly, though, they shared ideas about government and religion and learning and love, about everything and anything. Ideas lit up their minds. Books were their passion.

"I cannot live without books," Thomas Jefferson famously wrote in 1815. But he also admitted that he didn't need quite so many of them around his house anymore.

At eighty-one, John Adams was still studying philosophy just as eagerly as he had as a Harvard student, but now he realized that the teachings of the greatest philosophers could be "contained in four short Words, 'Be just and good.'"

As the years passed, the two friends grew frailer and their letters were exchanged less frequently. Each note became all the more precious.

"In wishing for your health and happiness, I am very selfish," Adams wrote in 1822, when he was eighty-six, "for I hope for more letters."

Adams got his wish. Their correspondence, as beautifully written as ever, continued for four more years.

July 4, 1826, fifty years after America announced its independence, was a day full of fireworks and parades and all the hoopla that half a century of freedom deserved.

John Adams was ninety years old and not to live another day. He lay dying in his own bed, surrounded by loved ones. After a lifetime full of words, he had strength for only a few more.

"Thomas Jefferson survives," he whispered.

Adams didn't know that his dear friend, also in his own bed, surrounded by his own loved ones, had passed away just a few hours earlier.

But maybe Adams was right.

Despite all that has changed in America since 1826, the homes of Jefferson and Adams are still crowded with visitors, the ideals they promoted are still inspiring others, and the nation they led still thrives.

Thomas Jefferson *does* survive, and John Adams, too. (He always liked to have the last word.)

HERE LIES
THOMAS
JEFFERSON

APRIL 13 1743
JULY 4 1826

J. ADAMS

born
OCT. 30 1735
died
JULY 4 1826

AFTERWORD

John Adams and Thomas Jefferson lived to be very, very old men. They outlived Washington, Hamilton, and George III. They outlasted Benjamin Franklin by more than twenty-five years and his son William by more than a dozen. They lived long enough to see that the country they had fought for—and fought over—was becoming a great nation.

Yet there were many more fights to come. It took another war, the Civil War, 1861–1865, to end the cruel institution of slavery, which had benefited George Washington, Thomas Jefferson, and, in his younger days, Benjamin Franklin. It was another hundred years, and another long, hard fight, before all Americans—no matter their color, religion, or gender—were protected by the Civil Rights Act of 1964.

"Remember the Ladies," Abigail Adams reminded her husband in 1776. "Do not put such unlimited powers into the hands of the Husbands." But John Adams forgot the ladies, and so did all the other founding fathers, at least when it came to giving political power to their mothers, wives, or daughters. Nearly 150 years would pass before women finally—after yet another long, hard struggle—won the right to vote, in 1920.

The founding fathers fought fiercely and stubbornly, and sometimes foolishly, for what they believed was right and just—or at least for what they believed was more right or more just than what their opponents were proposing. They created a nation where all people are free to disagree, respectfully and thoughtfully—or at the top of their lungs.

But the founding fathers aren't the only founders of America. They just started the job. The United States is still growing and changing, facing new challenges, confronting new problems. We are all still fighting the good fight.

NOTES AND SOURCES

⋆ ★ ⋆

George Washington vs. King George III: The War of the Georges

Page

4   "Nothing short of Independence . . .": George
      Washington letter to John Banister, April 21,
      1778. Founders Online, National Archives.

4   "I feel the justness . . .": King George III letter
      to Lord North, November 3, 1781. William
      Bodham Donne, ed., *The Correspondence of
      King George the Third with Lord North from 1768
      to 1783*.

8   "I am going to be mad . . .": Christopher
        Hibbert, *George III: A Personal History*, p. 261.

9   "I was summmoned . . .": George Washington's
        First Inaugural Address. Founders Online,
        National Archives.

14   "I do not think myself equal . . .": Journals
        of the Continental Congress, June 16, 1775.
        Library of Congress.

17   "Can a virtuous Man . . .": George Washington
        letter to George Fairfax, May 31, 1775. George
        Washington Papers, Library of Congress.

18   "unhappy and deluded": King George III
        address to Parliament, October 27, 1775. *The
        Parliamentary Register: Second Session of the Fourteenth
        Parliament of Great Britain.*

20   "I wish to Heaven . . .": George Washington
        letter to Lund Washington, December 17, 1776.
        Founders Online, National Archives.

22   "unhappy deluded Subjects in America . . .":
        "A Form of Prayer Issued by Special Command
        of His Majesty George III, London, 1776."

25   "The hands of France . . .": King George III
letter to Lord North, August 7, 1781. Donne,
ed., p. 381.

Benjamin Franklin vs. William Franklin: The Radical Father and the Conservative Son

28   "I am, Honoured Sir . . .": William Franklin letter
to Benjamin Franklin, September 1771. The
Papers of Benjamin Franklin (franklinpapers.org).

28   "I have lost my son . . .": Benjamin Franklin
letter to Richard Bache, June 2, 1779. The
Papers of Benjamin Franklin.

33   "I was surprised . . .": *The Autobiography of
Benjamin Franklin*, in *Franklin: Writings*, Library of
America, p. 1389.

36   "God helps them . . .": *Poor Richard's Almanack*
selection, in *Franklin: Writings*, Library of
America, p. 1201.

37   "Mr. Franklin's popularity . . .": Walter Isaacson,
Benjamin Franklin: An American Life, p. 173.

42   "inflaming the whole province . . .": H. W. Brands, *The First American: The Life and Times of Benjamin Franklin*, p. 473.

43   "I wish you were settled . . .": Benjamin Franklin letter to William Franklin, February 2, 1774. The Papers of Benjamin Franklin.

43   "Your popularity in this country . . .": William Franklin letter to Benjamin Franklin, May 3, 1774. The Papers of Benjamin Franklin.

44   "His Majesty may . . .": Isaacson, pp. 280–81.

45   "sitting in silence . . .": Isaacson, p. 292.

45   "Mr. Strahan . . .": Benjamin Franklin letter to William Strahan, July 5, 1775 (written but not sent). The Papers of Benjamin Franklin.

47   "Your father's face . . .": Benjamin Franklin letter to Sarah Franklin Bache, June 3, 1779. The Papers of Benjamin Franklin.

49   "It is His Majesty's . . .": Willard Sterne Randall, *A Little Revenge: Benjamin Franklin and His Son*, p. 353.

50   "Dear and Honoured Father . . .": William
      Franklin letter to Benjamin Franklin, July 22,
      1784. The Papers of Benjamin Franklin.

50   "I ought not to blame you . . .": Benjamin
      Franklin letter to William Franklin, August 16,
      1784. The Papers of Benjamin Franklin.

Alexander Hamilton vs. History: The Outsider

54   "I am a stranger . . .": Alexander Hamilton
      letter to John Laurens, January 8, 1780.
      Founders Online, National Archives.

54   "He hated every man . . .": Ron Chernow,
      Alexander Hamilton, p. 522.

59   "Apology is out of the question . . .": Alexander
      Hamilton, "Statement on Impending Duel with
      Aaron Burr," June 28–July 10, 1804. Founders
      Online, National Archives.

59   "I wish there was a war . . .": Alexander
      Hamilton letter to Edward Stevens, November
      11, 1769. Founders Online, National Archives.

62   "Good God! . . .": Alexander Hamilton letter to
      Royal Danish American Gazette, September 6, 1772.
      Founders Online, National Archives.

66   "[F]rom my soul . . .": George Washington
      letter to Continental Congress, December 23,
      1777. George Washington Papers, Library of
      Congress.

67   "For God's sake . . .": Alexander Hamilton letter
      to Colonel Henry E. Lutterloh, February 1778.
      Founders Online, National Archives.

69   "Something must be done . . .": George
      Washington letter to Continental Congress
      Camp Committee, January 29, 1778. Founders
      Online, National Archives.

72   "I conceived myself . . .": Alexander Hamilton
      letter to William Hamilton, May 2, 1797.
      Founders Online, National Archives.

74   "at the head of a faction . . .": Alexander
      Hamilton letter to Edward Carrington, May 26,
      1792. Founders Online, National Archives.

74   "guilty of high treason . . .": Thomas Jefferson
letter to James Madison, October 1, 1792.
Founders Online, National Archives.

77   "This is a mortal wound . . .": Chernow, p. 704.

77   "was enough to melt . . .": Chernow, p. 713.

John Adams vs. Thomas Jefferson: The Founding Frenemies

80   "His soul is poisoned . . .": John Adams letter
to Abigail Adams, December 26, 1793. The
Adams Family Papers, Massachusetts Historical
Society.

80   "I think it a part of his character . . .":
Thomas Jefferson letter to Benjamin Rush,
January 16, 1811. Founders Online, National
Archives.

86   "He means well . . .": Benjamin Franklin letter
to Robert Livingston, July 22, 1783. David
McCullough, *John Adams,* p. 285.

86   "I can feel for him . . .": John Adams letter to
      Edmund Jenings, July 20, 1782. The Adams
      Papers, Massachusetts Historical Society.

89   "The departure of your family . . .": Thomas
      Jefferson letter to John Adams, May 25, 1785.
      Lester J. Cappon, ed., *The Adams-Jefferson Letters*,
      p. 23.

90   "I shall really regret . . .": Abigail Adams letter
      to Lucy Cranch, May 7, 1785. Founders Online,
      National Archives.

92   "gross hyprocrite . . . ," etc.: McCullough, p. 537.

94   "I shall leave the State . . .": John Adams letter
      to F. A. Van der Kemp, December 28, 1800.
      James Grant, *John Adams: Party of One*, p. 427.

95   "A letter from you . . .": Thomas Jefferson letter
      to John Adams, January 21, 1812. Cappon,
      p. 291.

96   "Never mind . . .": John Adams letter to
      Thomas Jefferson, July 15, 1813. Cappon,
      p. 357.

97   "I cannot live without books . . .": Thomas
      Jefferson letter to John Adams, June 10, 1815.
      Cappon, p. 443.

97   "contained in four short Words . . .": John
      Adams letter to Thomas Jefferson, December
      12, 1816. Cappon, p. 499.

97   "In wishing for your health . . .": John Adams
      letter to Thomas Jefferson, June 11, 1822.
      Cappon, p. 580.

98   "Thomas Jefferson survives . . .": McCullough,
      p. 646.

Afterword

102   "Remember the Ladies . . .": Abigail Adams
      letter to John Adams, March 31, 1776. Adams
      Family Papers, Massachusetts Historical Society.

ONLINE RESOURCES

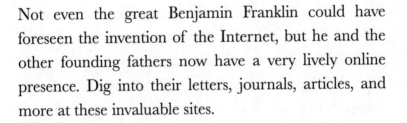

Not even the great Benjamin Franklin could have foreseen the invention of the Internet, but he and the other founding fathers now have a very lively online presence. Dig into their letters, journals, articles, and more at these invaluable sites.

The Adams Papers, Massachusetts Historical Society:
masshist.org

Founders Online, The National Archives:
foundersarchives.gov

The Library of Congress: loc.gov

The Papers of Benjamin Franklin: franklinpapers.org

SELECTED BIBLIOGRAPHY

✦★✦

"The past is never dead," wrote the American novelist William Faulkner. "It's not even past." Here are some of the fine books that I relied upon while working on *The Good Fight*. Each, in its own impressive way, proves Faulkner's point: the past lives on in our present, and our future, too.

Adams, William Howard. *The Paris Years of Thomas Jefferson*. New Haven: Yale University Press, 1997.

Brands, H. W. *The First American: The Life and Times of Benjamin Franklin*. New York: Doubleday, 2000.

Cappon, Lester J., ed. *The Adams-Jefferson Letters: The Complete Correspondence Between Thomas Jefferson and Abigail and John Adams.* Chapel Hill: University of North Carolina Press, 1959.

Chernow, Ron. *Alexander Hamilton.* New York: Penguin Books, 2004.

Chernow, Ron. *Washington: A Life.* New York: Penguin Books, 2010.

Ellis, Joseph J. *American Sphinx: The Character of Thomas Jefferson.* New York: Knopf, 1997.

Ellis, Joseph J. *His Excellency: George Washington.* New York: Knopf, 2004.

Fleming, Thomas. *Washington's Secret War: The Hidden History of Valley Forge.* Washington, DC: Smithsonian, 2005.

Franklin, Benjamin. *Franklin: Writings.* New York: Library of America, 1987.

Gordon-Reed, Annette. *The Hemingses of Monticello: An American Family.* New York: Norton, 2008.

Grant, James. *John Adams: Party of One.* New York: Farrar, Straus and Giroux, 2006.

Hamilton, Alexander. *Writings*. New York: Library of America, 2001.

Hibbert, Christopher. *George III: A Personal History*. New York: Basic Books, 1999.

Isaacson, Walter. *Benjamin Franklin: An American Life*. New York: Simon & Schuster, 2003.

McCullough, David. *John Adams*. New York: Simon & Schuster, 2001.

Randall, Willard Sterne. *A Little Revenge: Benjamin Franklin and His Son*. Boston: Little, Brown, 1984.